Food Truck Business Guide Book for Beginners
How to Start, Finance, Plan & Get Wholesale Equipment & Supplies

by Brian Mahoney

Table of Contents

Introduction

Part 1 Food Truck Business Overview

Part 2 Great reasons to start a food truck business

Part 3 How to Identify Your Food Truck Target Market

Part 4 How to create your food truck menu

Part 5 Food Truck Business Pricing Strategy

Part 6 Location Selection for Your Food Truck Business

Part 7 Food Truck Business Permits and Licenses

Part 8 Food Truck Health and Safety Regulations

Part 9 Choosing your Food Truck or Trailer

Table of Contents

Part 10 Equipment and Supplies for Your Food Truck Business

Part 11 Food Truck Websites for Equipment and Supplies

Part 12 Food Truck Business Marketing Plan

Part 13 Financing and Funding for Your Food Truck Business

Part 14 Food Truck Business Credit

Part 15 Dealing with Competition and other challenges to your Food Truck Business

Part 16 Food Truck Business Resources

Glossary of terms

Conclusion

Disclaimer

The information provided in Food Truck Business Guide Book for Beginners: How to Start, Finance, Plan & Get Wholesale Equipment & Supplies is for informational and educational purposes only. While every effort has been made to ensure the accuracy and reliability of the content, this book is not a substitute for professional advice. Readers are encouraged to consult with legal, financial, and business professionals before making any decisions related to starting or operating a food truck business.

The author and publisher make no guarantees or warranties regarding the outcomes or success of applying the information provided. Starting a business involves risks, and individual results will vary based on factors such as location, market conditions, and personal effort. The author and publisher disclaim any liability for loss, damage, or injury incurred as a result of using the information in this book.

By reading this book, you agree to take full responsibility for your decisions and actions. Please ensure you comply with all local, state, and federal regulations applicable to your business.

Let this guide be a resource to inspire and inform your entrepreneurial journey, but remember, your success depends on your determination, preparation, and adaptability.

Introduction

It's time to END MONEY WORRIES!

Welcome to...

Food Truck Business Guide Book for Beginners
How to Start, Finance, Plan & Get Wholesale Equipment & Supplies

by Brian Mahoney

Imagine you can have the knowledge you want, to start your business and live the Hassle Free All-American Lifestyle of Independence, Prosperity and Peace of Mind.

Get Excited because today you are about to discover...

Why now is a great time to start your food truck business

How to find your target market

How to create your food truck menu

What's the best pricing strategy for your business

How to select your location or locations

How to find wholesale prices on equipment and supplies

How to select the best food truck for your business and get it at wholesale prices

How to deal with competion

How to cut through government red tape and get your permits and licenses

How to form a LLC and protect your business

How to get Government Grants and Get up to 5 million dollars from the SBA

How to repair credit, raise your credit score, and get massive money in Business credit!

How to reach a Billion customers for FREE!

You have the right to restore a culture of the can-do spirit in your life. It's time to enjoy the financial security you and your family deserve... People are destroyed for lack of knowledge... So take advantage of this knowledge and let's get started today, making the rest of your life, the Best of your life!

PART 1
Food Truck Business Overview

The food truck industry is a dynamic and rapidly growing sector within the food and beverage industry. Here's an overview of this business:

Market Growth: The food truck industry has experienced significant growth in recent years, driven by factors such as changing consumer preferences for convenient and unique dining experiences, as well as lower overhead costs compared to traditional brick-and-mortar restaurants.

Diverse Cuisine: Food trucks offer a wide range of cuisines, from gourmet burgers and tacos to ethnic dishes like Thai, Mexican, and Mediterranean cuisine. This diversity appeals to a broad audience and allows for experimentation with different flavors and concepts.

Mobility and Flexibility: One of the key advantages of food trucks is their mobility. They can move to different locations based on demand, catering to events, festivals, office parks, and neighborhoods. This flexibility allows food truck owners to reach a larger customer base.

Lower Startup Costs: Compared to opening a traditional restaurant, starting a food truck business typically requires lower initial investment and operating costs. This makes it an attractive option for aspiring entrepreneurs looking to enter the food industry with limited resources.

Innovation and Creativity: Food trucks often innovate with their menu offerings, incorporating trends such as plant-based options, fusion cuisine, and unique flavor combinations. This creativity helps them stand out in a competitive market and attract loyal customers.

Challenges: Despite its popularity, the food truck industry also faces challenges such as regulation hurdles, competition for prime locations, changing seasons, and the need for efficient logistics and operations management.

Overall, the food truck industry offers entrepreneurs an exciting opportunity to showcase their culinary skills, connect with customers in a more casual setting, and contribute to the vibrant food culture in communities.

PART 2
Great reasons to start a food truck business

Low Initial Investment: Compared to opening a traditional restaurant, starting a food truck business typically requires lower initial capital. This can make it more accessible to entrepreneurs with limited funds.

Flexibility and Mobility: Food trucks offer the flexibility to change locations based on demand. You can explore different neighborhoods, events, or even follow seasonal trends to maximize your business opportunities.

Targeted Audience: Food trucks allow you to target specific demographics or events where there is a high demand for your type of food. For example, you can cater to office workers during lunch hours, festival-goers, or late-night crowds.

Creative Freedom: As a food truck owner, you have the creative freedom to experiment with diverse menus, fusion and unique recipes. This can help you stand out in a competitive market and attract food enthusiasts looking for new eating experiences.

Lower Overhead Costs: Operating a food truck typically involves lower overhead costs compared to a traditional restaurant. You can save on expenses like rent, and staffing, which can contribute to higher profit margins.

Community Engagement: Food trucks often foster a sense of community by interacting directly with customers in outdoor settings. This personal touch can build customer loyalty and generate positive word-of-mouth referrals.

Adaptability: Food trucks can adapt to changing trends and customer preferences more quickly than traditional restaurants. This agility allows you to stay relevant and capitalize on emerging food trends or seasonal ingredients.

Testing Ground for Ideas: A food truck can serve as a testing ground for new menu items, marketing strategies, and business concepts before scaling up to a larger operation. It provides valuable insights into what works best for your target audience.

Potential for Expansion: Successful food truck businesses can expand into multiple trucks, catering services, or even transition into a permanent restaurant if desired. This scalability offers long-term growth opportunities.

Passion and Creativity: For many entrepreneurs, running a food truck is a passion-driven endeavor that allows them to share their love for food with others. It's a platform to express creativity, culinary skills, and a entrepreneurial drive!

PART 3
How to Identify Your Food Truck Target Market

Identifying your target market for a food truck business involves understanding who your potential customers are and what their preferences, needs, and behaviors are. Here are steps to help you identify your target market:

Research Demographics: Start by researching the demographics of the area where you plan to operate your food truck. This includes factors such as age, gender, income level, occupation, education level, and family size.

Identify Customer Needs: Understand the needs and preferences of potential customers. Are they looking for quick and affordable meals, gourmet options, healthy food choices, or a specific cuisine type?

Research Competition: Study your competitors in the food truck industry. Identify who they are targeting and what makes them successful. This can give you insights into gaps in the market or opportunities to differentiate your offerings.

Conduct Surveys or Interviews: Engage with your target audience directly through surveys, interviews, or focus groups. Ask questions about their food preferences, dining habits, spending habits, and what would attract them to a food truck.

Use Social Media and Online Tools: Utilize social media platforms and online tools to gather data and insights about potential customers. Monitor conversations, trends, and feedback related to food trucks and similar businesses.

Consider Location: The location of your food truck can also influence your target market. For example, if you park near offices, your target market might be working professionals looking for quick lunch options. If you park near parks or tourist attractions, your target market may include families, tourists, or outdoor enthusiasts.

Create Customer Avatar: Based on the information gathered, create customer avatars that represents your target audience. Include details such as demographics, preferences, behaviors, challenges, and goals. This helps you tailor your marketing strategies and offerings effectively.

By following these steps and continuously gathering feedback and data, you can refine your understanding of your target market and tailor your food truck business to meet their needs and preferences.

PART 4

How to create your food truck menu

Planning a menu for your food truck business involves several key steps to ensure success. Here's a guide to help you plan your food truck menu effectively:

Research Your Market:

Understand the preferences and tastes of your target customers.

Identify popular food trends and cuisines in your area.

Consider dietary preferences such as vegetarian, vegan, gluten-free, etc.

Define Your Concept:

Decide on the type of cuisine or theme for your food truck (e.g., Mexican, BBQ, burgers, fusion).

Determine if you want to focus on a specific meal (e.g., breakfast, lunch, snacks) or offer a full menu.

Create a Core Menu:

Develop a list of signature dishes that represent your concept and appeal to your target market.

Include a variety of items such as main dishes, sides, desserts, and beverages.

Ensure your menu has a good balance of flavors, textures, and dietary options.

Consider Pricing Strategy:

Determine the price range for your menu items based on ingredient costs, competition, and target customers' willingness to pay.

Offer value combos or meal deals to attract customers and increase sales.

Test and Refine:

Conduct taste tests and get feedback from friends, family, and potential customers.

Make adjustments to the menu based on feedback and popularity of dishes.

Seasonal and Special Items:
Consider offering seasonal specials or limited-time menu items to create excitement and attract repeat customers.
Incorporate local ingredients or seasonal flavors to stay relevant and appeal to seasonal trends.

Menu Presentation:
Design an eye-catching menu board or digital menu that is easy to read and understand.
Use enticing descriptions and high-quality images to showcase your dishes and tempt customers.

Operational Considerations:
Ensure your menu is manageable in terms of preparation, cooking, and serving times.
Plan for ingredient sourcing, storage, and inventory management to maintain menu consistency and quality.

By following these steps and continuously evaluating your menu based on customer feedback and market trends, you can create a compelling and successful menu for your food truck business.

If you are still feeling a little lost, here's a standard food truck menu that includes a variety of popular items that can get you started:

Main Dishes:
Cheeseburger: Classic beef patty, cheese, lettuce, tomato, onion, and special sauce on a brioche bun.
Chicken Tacos: Grilled chicken, lettuce, salsa, cheese, and sour cream in soft corn tortillas.
Veggie Wrap: Grilled vegetables, hummus, mixed greens, and feta cheese in a whole wheat wrap.

Sides:

French Fries: Crispy golden fries served with ketchup or aioli dipping sauce.

Onion Rings: Beer-battered onion rings fried to perfection and served with ranch dressing.

Caesar Salad: Romaine lettuce, croutons, Parmesan cheese, and Caesar dressing.

Specialty Items:

BBQ Pulled Pork Sandwich: Slow-cooked pulled pork in tangy BBQ sauce, served on a toasted bun with coleslaw.

Fish Tacos: Beer-battered fish, cabbage slaw, avocado crema, and salsa in soft flour tortillas.

Falafel Bowl: Crispy falafel balls, tabbouleh salad, hummus, and tahini sauce over quinoa.

Desserts:

Churros: Fried dough dusted with cinnamon sugar, served with chocolate dipping sauce.

Ice Cream Sandwich: Vanilla ice cream sandwiched between two chocolate chip cookies.

Fruit Salad: Fresh seasonal fruits served chilled with a drizzle of honey-lime dressing.

Beverages:

Soft Drinks: Coke, Sprite, Diet Coke, and other soda options.

Iced Tea: Sweetened or unsweetened iced tea with lemon slices.

Bottled Water: Still or sparkling bottled water.

This menu offers a mix of classic favorites like burgers and tacos, along with some specialty items for variety. You can adjust the menu based on your specific concept, target audience, and available ingredients. Don't forget to include pricing and attractive descriptions on your menu board to entice customers!

PART 5
Food Truck Business Pricing Strategy

A good pricing strategy for your food truck business can depend on various factors such as your target market, competition, costs, and value proposition. Here are some pricing strategies you can consider:

Penetration pricing: this is a marketing strategy used by businesses to attract customers to a new product or service by offering a lower price during its initial offering. The lower price helps a new product or service penetrate the market and attract customers away from competitors.

Cost-Plus Pricing: Calculate all your costs (ingredients, labor, overhead, etc.) and add a markup to determine your selling price. This ensures you cover your expenses and make a profit.

Value-Based Pricing: Set your prices based on the perceived value of your food. If you offer unique or high-quality dishes, you can price them higher than standard items.

Competitive Pricing: Research your competitors' prices and set yours either slightly lower, at par, or higher depending on your positioning and unique selling points.

Bundle Pricing: Offer meal deals or combos to encourage customers to spend more. For example, a combo meal with a main dish, side, and drink at a discounted price compared to buying each item separately.

Seasonal Pricing: Adjust your prices based on seasons or events. For instance, you can have special promotions or discounts during holidays or festivals to attract more customers.

Psychological Pricing: Use pricing techniques like setting prices just below a round number ($9.99 instead of $10) or highlighting discounts (e.g., "20% off") to make your prices more attractive.

Dynamic Pricing: Adjust prices based on demand, time of day, or other factors. For example, you can offer lower prices during off-peak hours to attract more customers.

Tiered Pricing: Offer different pricing tiers with varying levels of service or portions. This allows customers to choose what fits their budget and preferences.

Consider experimenting with different pricing strategies and monitor their impact on sales and profitability. Customer feedback and market trends can also guide your pricing decisions over time.

PART 6
Location Selection for Your Food Truck Business

Selecting a good location for your food truck business is crucial for its success. Here are some steps to help you choose the right location:

Understand Your Target Market: Identify your target customers, their preferences, and where they are likely to be. Consider factors such as demographics, lifestyle, and eating habits.

Research High-Traffic Areas: Look for areas with high foot traffic, such as business districts, shopping centers, tourist spots, parks, and event venues. These locations can attract a steady flow of potential customers.

Consider Competition: Evaluate the presence of competitors in the area. While some competition can be healthy, too much might saturate the market. Choose a location where you can stand out or offer something unique.

Check Zoning Regulations: Ensure that the location you choose complies with local zoning regulations and permits for food trucks. Some areas may have restrictions on where food trucks can operate.

Assess Parking and Accessibility: Consider the availability of parking space for your food truck and ensure ease of access for both customers and your truck.

Evaluate Visibility and Signage: Opt for a location with good visibility to attract passing traffic. Invest in eye-catching signage to attract customers and make your presence known.

Review Costs: Evaluate the costs associated with operating in different locations, including rent or fees, utilities, and other expenses. Balance these costs with the potential foot traffic and revenue.

Test Multiple Locations: Consider testing your food truck in different locations on different days to gather data on customer preferences, sales, and foot traffic before committing to a long-term location.

By following these steps and carefully considering factors like target market, competition, regulations, accessibility, visibility, and costs, you can select a good location that maximizes your food truck business's potential for success.

PART 7

Food Truck Business Permits and Licenses

Obtaining permits and licenses for your food truck business is a crucial step in ensuring compliance with local regulations and operating legally. Here are the general steps you should follow:

Research Local Requirements: Start by researching the specific permits and licenses required for operating a food truck in your city or county. Regulations can vary significantly depending on your location.

Contact the Local Health Department: Reach out to your local health department to understand the food safety regulations and requirements for operating a food truck. They can provide information on necessary certifications and inspections.

Apply for a Health Permit: Obtain a health permit, also known as a food handler's permit or food establishment permit, which demonstrates that your food truck meets health and safety standards.

Business License: Apply for a business license or a mobile food vending license from your city or county government. This license allows you to legally operate a business within the area.

Food Handler Certifications: Ensure that all employees handling food in your food truck have the required food handler certifications. These certifications may involve completing a food safety course and passing an exam.

Zoning and Parking Permits: Check zoning regulations to ensure that you can park and operate your food truck in specific areas. You may need parking permits or approvals from property owners or local authorities.

Fire Safety Permit: Depending on your location and the size of your food truck, you may need a fire safety permit to ensure compliance with fire codes and safety measures.

Other Permits and Inspections: In addition to the above, you may need other permits and inspections, such as propane or gas permits for cooking equipment, signage permits, and wastewater disposal permits.

Submit Applications and Fees: Prepare and submit all required applications along with any necessary fees. Keep track of deadlines and follow up on the status of your applications.

Attend Inspections: Once your applications are approved, schedule and attend any required inspections to ensure that your food truck meets all regulatory requirements.

It's important to stay updated on any changes in regulations and renew your permits and licenses as required to avoid penalties or disruptions to your business operations. Consulting with legal and regulatory experts can also be helpful in navigating the permit and licensing process effectively.

PART 8
Food Truck Health and Safety Regulations

Learning about health and safety regulations for your food truck business is crucial for ensuring compliance and the well-being of your customers. Here are some steps you can take to learn about these regulations:

Research Government Websites: Visit the official websites of government agencies responsible for regulating food safety in your area. This could include the Food and Drug Administration (FDA) or the Department of Health. These websites often provide detailed information on food safety requirements, regulations, and guidelines specific to food trucks.

Attend Workshops or Seminars: Look for workshops, seminars, or training programs conducted by health departments or industry associations. These events can provide valuable insights into health and safety practices, regulations, and compliance requirements for food truck operators.

Consult with Health Inspectors: Schedule a meeting or consultation with health inspectors or regulatory officials in your area. They can provide you with specific information about the regulations you need to follow, answer your questions, and guide you through the process of obtaining necessary permits and licenses.

Join Industry Associations: Consider joining industry associations or organizations related to food truck operations. These associations often offer resources, guidance, and networking opportunities that can help you stay informed about health and safety regulations and best practices.

Online Courses and Resources: Explore online courses, webinars, and resources focused on food safety and regulations for food businesses. Many reputable organizations and platforms offer courses specifically tailored to food truck operators.

Consult Legal and Regulatory Experts: If you have specific questions or concerns about health and safety regulations, consider consulting with legal experts or regulatory consultants who specialize in food industry regulations. They can provide personalized guidance based on your location and business needs.

By taking these steps and staying proactive in learning about health and safety regulations, you can ensure that your food truck business meets all necessary requirements and operates safely and legally.

PART 9
Choosing your Food Truck or Trailer

Choosing the right truck or trailer for your food truck business is crucial for your success. Here are some steps to help you make the right choice:

Define Your Menu and Equipment Needs: Start by defining your menu and the equipment you'll need to prepare and serve your dishes. This will help determine the size and layout requirements of your truck or trailer.

Consider Your Budget: Determine how much you're willing to invest in your food truck or trailer. This will narrow down your options and help you focus on vehicles that are within your budget.

Size and Layout: Choose a truck or trailer that provides enough space for your kitchen equipment, storage, and workspace. Consider factors like the number of staff members who will be working inside and how much standing room customers will need.

Mobility Requirements: Consider where you plan to operate your food truck. If you'll be navigating tight urban streets, a smaller truck may be more practical. For larger events or rural locations, a bigger truck or trailer might be suitable.

Condition and Maintenance: Whether you're buying new or used, inspect the condition of the truck or trailer thoroughly. Consider ongoing maintenance costs and the availability of parts and service in your area.

Compliance and Regulations: Ensure that the vehicle you choose complies with health and safety regulations, including those related to food handling, fire safety, and vehicle inspections. Check with your local health department and regulatory agencies for specific requirements.

Customization Options: Depending on your menu and branding, you may want to customize the interior and exterior of your truck or trailer. Consider customization options that align with your business goals and customer experience.

Insurance and Financing: Research insurance options for food trucks or trailers and consider financing options if you're not purchasing outright. Factor in insurance costs and financing terms when making your decision.

By carefully considering these factors, you can choose the right truck or trailer that meets your business needs and sets you up for success in the food truck industry.

Websites for Finding a Discount Vehicle

FoodTruckEmpire.com

FoodTruckEmpire.com offers a wide range of new and used food trucks for sale. They feature listings from various sellers across the United States, making it easy to compare prices and find discounts on food trucks that fit your budget and requirements.

UsedVending.com

UsedVending.com specializes in selling used food trucks, trailers, and other vending equipment. They have a large inventory of discounted trucks from different brands and sellers. You can browse through their listings and contact sellers directly to negotiate prices.

FoodTruckForSale.com

FoodTruckForSale.com is a marketplace for buying and selling new and used food trucks. They offer discounts on pre-owned trucks and provide detailed listings with photos, specifications, and seller contact information. You can search for trucks based on location, price range, and other criteria.

RoamingHunger.com

Roaming Hunger is a platform that connects food truck buyers with sellers. While they primarily focus on helping customers find food trucks for events and catering, they also list discounted trucks for sale. You can use their search filters to narrow down options based on your budget and location.

Craigslist.org

Craigslist is a popular online classifieds platform where you can find a variety of items for sale, including food trucks. While listings on Craigslist may vary by location and availability, it's worth checking regularly for discounted trucks and negotiating directly with sellers.

These are not the only websites, but do offer a range of options, to get your started finding discounted trucks for your food truck business. Be sure to thoroughly research each listing, inspect the vehicles in person if possible, and negotiate prices to get the best deal.

PART 10

Equipment and Supplies for Your Food Truck Business

Starting a food truck business requires specific equipment and supplies to ensure smooth operations and the ability to serve high-quality food. Here's a list of essential items you'll need:

Food Truck Vehicle: This is the core of your business, and it should be equipped with cooking and storage facilities. Consider factors like size, mobility, and layout when choosing a food truck.

Cooking Equipment:

Griddle or grill for cooking burgers, sandwiches, and other items.
Deep fryer for frying foods like French fries, chicken tenders, or fried seafood.
Range or stove for cooking soups, stews, and sauces.
Oven for baking or roasting.
Microwave for quick heating or cooking of certain items.
Refrigeration units for storing perishable ingredients.

Food Preparation Equipment:

Cutting boards, knives, and utensils for food prep.
Mixing bowls, pots, and pans for cooking.
Food processors or blenders for making sauces, dips, or smoothies.
Slicers and dicers for efficiently preparing ingredients.

Service and Display Equipment:

Serving counter or window for customer interactions.
Display cases or shelves for showcasing menu items.
Cash register or POS system for transactions.
Menu boards or signs for displaying offerings and prices.

Storage and Organization:
Shelving units and cabinets for storing ingredients, utensils, and supplies.
Storage containers and bins for keeping food fresh and organized.
Trash cans and recycling bins for waste management.

Safety and Sanitation:
Fire extinguisher and first aid kit for emergencies.
Handwashing sink and sanitizing stations for food safety.
Cleaning supplies such as sanitizers, detergents, and trash bags.
Food-grade gloves and hairnets for food handling hygiene.

Generator or Power Source: Ensure you have a reliable power source to run your equipment, especially if operating in locations without access to electrical hookups.

Menu-Specific Equipment: Depending on your menu, you may need specialized equipment like a pizza oven, waffle maker, or ice cream machine.

Disposable and Serving Supplies:
Disposable plates, utensils, and cups.
Napkins, paper towels, and wipes for cleaning and customer use.
Takeaway containers and bags for serving food to go.

Marketing and Branding Materials: Business cards, flyers, menus, and branded merchandise to promote your food truck and attract customers.

It's crucial to research local regulations and health codes to ensure compliance with requirements related to equipment, food handling, and safety standards. Additionally, consider factors like space limitations, budget constraints, and menu complexity when selecting equipment and supplies for your food truck business.

Food Truck Websites for Equipment and Supplies

WebstaurantStore.com

Summary: WebstaurantStore is a comprehensive online restaurant supply store offering a wide range of equipment, supplies, and furniture for food service businesses. They have competitive prices, a vast selection of products, and fast shipping options, making them a popular choice for food truck owners.

Restaurant Depot.com

Summary: Restaurant Depot is a membership-based wholesale supplier catering to restaurants, food trucks, and other foodservice establishments. They offer bulk discounts on a variety of products, including food items, equipment, disposables, and cleaning supplies. Membership is required to shop at Restaurant Depot.

KaTom.com

Summary: KaTom Restaurant Supply is a trusted supplier of commercial kitchen equipment, smallwares, and restaurant supplies. They have a user-friendly website with a wide range of products from leading brands. KaTom offers competitive pricing, excellent customer service, and quick delivery options.

Ace Mart.com

Summary: Ace Mart is a reliable source for restaurant and foodservice equipment, supplies, and furniture. They cater to various industries, including food trucks, with a diverse selection of products at competitive prices. Ace Mart also provides personalized customer support and fast shipping services.

TigerChef.com

Summary: TigerChef is an online restaurant supply store offering a wide array of products for commercial kitchens and food trucks. They have a user-friendly website, competitive pricing, and a large inventory of equipment, smallwares, and consumables. TigerChef also provides resources and guides for restaurant owners.

These websites are reputable sources for purchasing equipment, supplies, and other essentials for your food truck business. It's recommended to compare prices, read customer reviews, and consider shipping costs and delivery times before making purchases.

PART 11
Food Truck Websites for Equipment and Supplies

WebstaurantStore.com

Summary: WebstaurantStore is a comprehensive online restaurant supply store offering a wide range of equipment, supplies, and furniture for food service businesses. They have competitive prices, a vast selection of products, and fast shipping options, making them a popular choice for food truck owners.

Restaurant Depot.com

Summary: Restaurant Depot is a membership-based wholesale supplier catering to restaurants, food trucks, and other foodservice establishments. They offer bulk discounts on a variety of products, including food items, equipment, disposables, and cleaning supplies. Membership is required to shop at Restaurant Depot.

KaTom.com

Summary: KaTom Restaurant Supply is a trusted supplier of commercial kitchen equipment, smallwares, and restaurant supplies. They have a user-friendly website with a wide range of products from leading brands. KaTom offers competitive pricing, excellent customer service, and quick delivery options.

Ace Mart.com

Summary: Ace Mart is a reliable source for restaurant and foodservice equipment, supplies, and furniture. They cater to various industries, including food trucks, with a diverse selection of products at competitive prices. Ace Mart also provides personalized customer support and fast shipping services.

TigerChef.com

Summary: TigerChef is an online restaurant supply store offering a wide array of products for commercial kitchens and food trucks. They have a user-friendly website, competitive pricing, and a large inventory of equipment, smallwares, and consumables. TigerChef also provides resources and guides for restaurant owners.

These websites are reputable sources for purchasing equipment, supplies, and other essentials for your food truck business. It's recommended to compare prices, read customer reviews, and consider shipping costs and delivery times before making purchases.

PART 12
Food Truck Business Marketing Plan

Developing a marketing plan for your food truck business involves several key steps to effectively reach your target audience and promote your offerings. Here's a structured approach to creating a marketing plan:

Market Research:
Identify your target market (e.g., demographics, preferences, behaviors).

Analyze your competitors (e.g., their offerings, pricing, marketing strategies).

Unique Selling Proposition (USP):
Determine what sets your food truck apart from competitors.

Highlight your USP in your marketing efforts to attract customers.

Goals and Objectives:
Set specific, measurable, achievable, relevant, and time-bound (SMART) goals.

Examples of goals could include increasing sales by a certain percentage, expanding to new locations, or building brand awareness.

Marketing Strategies:
Define your marketing mix (Product, Price, Place, Promotion).

Product: Describe your food offerings, menu variations, and specials.

Price: Determine your pricing strategy (e.g., competitive pricing, premium pricing, value pricing).

Place: Identify locations where you'll operate your food truck and consider partnerships with events or businesses.

Promotion: Outline how you'll promote your food truck (e.g., social media, email marketing, partnerships, events).

Budget Allocation:
Allocate a budget for each marketing strategy based on your goals and resources.

Consider both online and offline marketing channels and tactics. Later in this book we will cover the massive marketing advantage using YouTube!

Implementation Plan:
Create a timeline for implementing each marketing strategy.

Assign responsibilities to team members or external partners.

Measurement and Analysis:
Define key performance indicators (KPIs) to track the success of your marketing efforts (e.g., sales growth, customer acquisition cost, social media engagement).

Regularly measure and analyze the results to make data-driven decisions and adjust your marketing plan as needed.

Feedback and Improvement:
Gather feedback from customers, employees, and stakeholders.

Use feedback to improve your offerings and marketing strategies continuously.

By following these steps, you can develop a comprehensive marketing plan that helps promote your food truck business effectively and achieve your business objectives.

PART 13

Financing and Funding for Your Food Truck Business

Securing financing and funding options for your food truck business involves exploring various sources of capital to fund your startup costs, operations, and growth. Here are some common financing options and strategies you can consider:

Paypal Credit loan: If you have a paypal account, almost anybody can qualify for at least $1,500 and get charged no interest if paid in full in 6 months on purchases of $99 or more when you check out with Paypal credit. I have personally used this for several large purchases. It is a revolving line of credit that stays on your regular paypal account to use in addion to their regular credit card offers. The one draw back is the merchant has to accept paypal.

Personal Savings: Using your own savings or personal assets is one of the simplest ways to finance your food truck business. This can include money from savings accounts, retirement funds, or the sale of personal assets.

Family and Friends: You can seek financial support from family members or friends who believe in your business idea. This can be in the form of loans or investments.

Microloans: Microloans are small loans typically offered by nonprofit organizations, community development financial institutions (CDFIs), or online lenders. They are suitable for businesses with modest financing needs.

Angel Investors: Angel investors are individuals or groups who provide capital to startups in exchange for equity or convertible debt. They often bring valuable expertise and networking opportunities.

Venture Capitalists (VCs): Venture capitalists invest in high-growth startups with the potential for significant returns. They typically provide larger amounts of capital but also require a significant equity stake in your business.

Equipment Financing: If you need to purchase or lease equipment for your food truck, you can explore equipment financing options. This allows you to spread the cost of equipment over time while using it to generate revenue.

Bank Loans: Traditional bank loans are a common source of financing for small businesses. You can apply for a business loan based on your creditworthiness, business plan, and collateral.

Business Credit: Business credit refers to a company's creditworthiness and financial reputation in the eyes of lenders and suppliers. It is separate from personal credit and is based on the business's payment history, credit utilization, and other financial factors. Building strong business credit is crucial for obtaining loans, credit lines, and favorable terms from vendors, helping businesses to grow and thrive financially.

Crowdfunding: Crowdfunding is a fundraising method that involves collecting small contributions from a large number of individuals or organizations to finance a project or venture. It typically takes place on online platforms dedicated to crowdfunding, where creators showcase their projects and invite people to contribute financially. Crowdfunding allows creators to access capital without traditional sources like banks or investors, while supporters can participate in projects they believe in and often receive rewards or incentives in return for their contributions.

Grants: Grants are non-repayable funds provided by governments, foundations, or organizations to individuals, businesses, or nonprofits for specific purposes such as research, education, or community development. Unlike loans, grants do not need to be repaid, making them a valuable source of funding for projects or initiatives with social, environmental, or economic benefits. Grant recipients are usually required to meet certain criteria, such as demonstrating the potential impact of their project and adhering to grant guidelines and reporting requirements.

Small Business Administration (SBA) Loans: Small Business Administration (SBA) loans are financial products offered by the U.S. Small Business Administration to support small businesses in various industries. These loans are designed to provide affordable financing for starting, expanding, or acquiring small businesses, offering lower interest rates and longer repayment terms than traditional loans. SBA loans are available through participating lenders and come with specific eligibility criteria and application processes tailored to different types of businesses and their funding needs. These business loans can reach a maximum of 5 million dollars!

When choosing the right financing option for your food truck business, consider factors such as the amount of capital needed, your creditworthiness, repayment terms, interest rates, and the impact on your ownership and control of the business. It's also important to have a solid business plan and financial projections to demonstrate your business's viability to potential lenders or investors.

Later in this book We will cover Business credit, crowdfunding, government grants, & small business administration guaranteed loans in more detail.

PART 14
Food Truck Business Credit

How to get business credit for your food truck business

Incorporate Your Business: Register your food truck business as a legal entity, such as a corporation or LLC (Limited Liability Company). This separates your personal and business finances, which is crucial for building business credit.

Get an Employer Identification Number (EIN): Obtain an EIN from the IRS, which is like a social security number for your business. This is necessary for opening business bank accounts and applying for credit.

Open a Business Bank Account: Use your EIN to open a business bank account in your food truck's name. Keep your business finances separate from personal finances to build a strong credit history.

Apply for a D-U-N-S Number: Register for a D-U-N-S Number from Dun & Bradstreet, a credit reporting agency that specializes in business credit. This unique identifier is often required when applying for business credit.

Establish Trade Lines: Work with vendors and suppliers who report payments to business credit bureaus. Consistently pay bills on time to build a positive credit history.

Apply for a Business Credit Card: Look for business credit cards that offer rewards and benefits suited to your food truck business. Make regular, on-time payments to boost your credit score.

Monitor Your Credit Reports: Regularly check your business credit reports from major credit bureaus like Dun & Bradstreet, Experian, and Equifax. Address any errors or discrepancies promptly.

Build Relationships with Lenders: As your business credit history grows, establish relationships with lenders and financial institutions. This can lead to opportunities for larger credit lines and better financing options.

Use Credit Wisely: Be strategic with your credit utilization and avoid maxing out credit lines. Maintain a good payment history and manage your debts responsibly.

PART 15

Dealing with Competition and other challenges to your Food Truck Business

Dealing with competition, managing seasonal changes, and addressing weather impacts are important aspects of running a successful food truck business. Here are some strategies you can consider:

Competitive Analysis:

Identify your direct and indirect competitors in the area. Direct competitors are other food trucks or vendors offering similar cuisine, while indirect competitors are restaurants or other eateries.

Analyze their offerings, pricing, customer base, and marketing strategies.

Differentiate your food truck by offering unique menu items, special promotions, excellent customer service, or a memorable brand experience.

Customer Engagement and Loyalty:

Build strong relationships with your customers through social media, email marketing, loyalty programs, and customer feedback. More detailed social media marketing training will be covered in other parts of this book.

Offer incentives such as discounts, freebies, or loyalty points to encourage repeat business.

Collect customer data and use it to personalize your offerings and promotions.

Seasonal Adaptation:

Adjust your menu according to seasonal trends and local preferences. For example, offer refreshing drinks and salads in summer and hearty soups and warm beverages in winter.

Promote seasonal specials and limited-time offers to attract customers during specific times of the year.

Plan ahead for seasonal fluctuations in foot traffic and adjust your staffing and inventory accordingly.

Weather Contingency Plans:

Monitor weather forecasts regularly and have contingency plans in place for extreme weather conditions such as storms, heatwaves, or heavy rain.

Invest in equipment and infrastructure that can withstand weather challenges, such as awnings, heaters, or cooling systems.

Consider alternative locations or events during inclement weather to maintain business continuity.

Diversification and Flexibility:

Diversify your revenue streams by catering events, partnering with local businesses, or offering delivery services.

Stay flexible with your menu and operations to adapt to changing customer demands, market trends, and external factors like weather or competition.

Continuous Improvement:

Regularly evaluate your performance, gather feedback from customers and staff, and make data-driven decisions to improve your offerings and operations.

Stay updated with industry trends, innovations, and best practices to remain competitive and relevant in the market.

By implementing these strategies, you can effectively manage competition, navigate seasonal variations, and mitigate weather impacts to optimize your food truck business's success.

PART 16
Food Truck Business Resources

Here are some resources and materials to help you start a food truck business:

Websites and Online Guides:

National Food Truck Association (NFTA) website: Provides resources, guidelines, and information for starting and operating a food truck business.

Food Truck Empire: Offers articles, guides, and resources for aspiring food truck entrepreneurs.

Small Business Administration (SBA) Guide to Starting a Food Truck Business: Provides step-by-step guidance on planning, launching, and managing a food truck business.

Courses and Workshops:

Local business development centers or chambers of commerce may offer workshops or courses specifically for food truck entrepreneurs.

Online platforms like Udemy, Coursera, or Skillshare may have courses on starting a food truck business.

Industry Publications and Magazines:

"Mobile Cuisine Magazine": Covers news, trends, and tips for the mobile food industry.

"Food Truck Operator Magazine": Provides insights, case studies, and best practices for food truck operators.

Networking and Community Events:

Attend food truck festivals, industry conferences, and networking events to connect with other food truck owners and learn from their experiences.
Join online forums and social media groups for food truck entrepreneurs to ask questions, share ideas, and get support.

Remember to research local regulations, obtain necessary permits and licenses, create a solid business plan, and develop a unique selling proposition (USP) for your food truck to stand out in the market.

Glossary of Terms for Food Truck Business Guide Book for Beginners

Business License – Official permission to operate a business in a specific area.

Commissary Kitchen – A licensed commercial kitchen used for food preparation and storage.

Food Cost Percentage – A measure of food costs relative to menu pricing.

Health Permit – A certification ensuring compliance with food safety regulations.

Point-of-Sale (POS) System – Technology used to process customer payments.

Commercial Vehicle Insurance **– Insurance covering food trucks against accidents** and liabilities.

Branding – Creating a unique identity for your food truck business.

Menu Engineering – Strategic planning of menu items to maximize profitability.

Mobile Food Unit (MFU) – A motorized or towed vehicle for preparing and serving food.

Event Catering – Providing food services for special events via a food truck.

Start-Up Costs – Initial expenses to launch a food truck business.

Food Truck Festival – A public event featuring multiple food trucks.

Overhead Costs – Fixed and variable expenses, excluding food and labor.

Operating Hours – Specific times your food truck serves customers.

Vendor Permit – Authorization to sell food in public areas.

Truck Wrap – A custom design applied to a food truck for advertising.

Crowdfunding – Raising start-up capital via online donations.

Wholesale Suppliers – Vendors offering bulk discounts on equipment and supplies.

Service Window – The area where customers order and receive food.

Prepping Station – A designated area for food preparation.

Grease Trap – Equipment capturing fats and oils from food waste.

Generator – A portable device providing electrical power to the food truck.

Inventory Management – Tracking stock levels to avoid shortages.

Fleet – A group of food trucks operated by one owner.

Profit Margin – The percentage of revenue remaining after expenses.

Licensing Fees – Costs to acquire necessary business permits.

Mobile POS – A portable system for taking orders and processing payments.

Daily Sales Report – A summary of sales and income for the day.

Route Planning – Strategizing locations and times for food truck service.

Kitchen Workflow – The organization of tasks for efficient food preparation.

Social Media Marketing – Using platforms like Instagram to attract customers.

Sanitation Standards – Hygiene practices required by law for food handling.

Truck Lease – Renting a food truck instead of purchasing one.

Customer Demographics – Characteristics of your target audience.

Food Truck Park – A designated area where multiple food trucks operate.

Employee Training – Teaching staff food safety and customer service skills.

Specialty Menu – A unique selection of food items defining your brand.

Seasonal Demand – Fluctuations in customer interest based on seasons.

Cash Flow – The net amount of cash moving in and out of the business.

Brand Ambassadors – Loyal customers promoting your business by word-of-mouth.

Market Research – Gathering data on competitors and customer preferences.

Food Truck Association – A group offering resources and advocacy for operators.

Soft Opening – A trial run before the official launch of the food truck.

Permitting Process – Steps to acquire legal authorization for operation.

Vendor Relationships – Partnerships with suppliers for consistent inventory.

Digital Menu Board – Electronic displays for showcasing food items.

Local Ordinances – City or county laws affecting food truck operations.

Eco-Friendly Packaging – Biodegradable or recyclable food containers.

Revenue Streams – Sources of income like catering or regular street service.

Customer Loyalty Program – Incentives encouraging repeat visits.

World Food Trucks

World Food Trucks in Kissimmee, Florida, is a vibrant food truck park offering a diverse range of global cuisines with a strong focus on Latin American flavors. Located at 5811 W. Irlo Bronson Memorial Highway, just across from Old Town and Fun Spot, it features over 50 food trucks, with plans to expand to more than 100. Open daily from noon until late at night, the park serves dishes from Puerto Rico, Mexico, Venezuela, and beyond, often with a unique twist.

Popular items include mofongo, empanadas, tacos, and fusion dishes like smoked rice with pulled pork. The park also offers a carnival-like atmosphere with desserts such as mini donuts, funnel cakes, and ice cream. World Food Trucks frequently hosts events like karaoke nights, making it an engaging destination for families and food lovers alike

For more details, visit their official website or explore their YouTube channel for food truck profiles.

https://www.worldfoodtrucks.com/

Food Trucks Heaven

Food Trucks Heaven in Kissimmee, Florida, is a vibrant spot for food enthusiasts and families. Located behind the Main Gate Flea Market at 5403 W Irlo Bronson Memorial Highway, it features a variety of gourmet food trucks offering diverse cuisines, from artisanal tacos and Cuban sandwiches to gourmet desserts like churros and ice cream. The atmosphere is lively, often enhanced by live music and family-friendly entertainment. Visitors can enjoy their meals in outdoor seating areas while soaking in the fun, community-oriented vibe

It's open daily, typically from noon to 10:30 PM, with extended hours on weekends. Parking is convenient, and the venue is known for its eclectic mix of flavors and excellent service

For more details, you can visit their official website or call (407) 305-3624

https://foodtrucksheaven.com/

Conclusion

Embarking on a journey in the food truck business is an exciting and rewarding endeavor, combining culinary creativity with entrepreneurial spirit. Throughout this book, we've explored every critical step needed to establish, manage, and grow a successful food truck operation. From understanding your target market and crafting the perfect menu to navigating licenses, health regulations, and competition, this guide has been designed to equip you with practical knowledge and actionable insights.

The food truck industry offers endless opportunities for innovation and personal expression. However, success requires more than just passion for cooking; it demands strategic planning, adaptability, and a willingness to learn. As you move forward, leverage the resources, tips, and strategies outlined in these chapters to overcome challenges and stand out in a competitive market.

Remember, your food truck is more than a business—it's a representation of your brand, vision, and love for sharing great food. With dedication and the right approach, your food truck can become not just a source of income, but a mobile hub for community, connection, and culinary delight.

The road ahead may have its challenges, but the rewards are worth it. Take your first step, stay committed to your goals, and let your food truck journey begin. The possibilities are endless, and success is just around the corner!

Finally, if you enjoyed this book, please take the time to share your thoughts and post a review on Amazon. It'd be greatly appreciated!

Many Thanks,

Brian Mahoney

You might also be interested in:

How To Get Money for Small Business Start Up:

How to Get Massive Money from Crowdfunding, Government Grants and Government Loans

By Ramsey Colwell

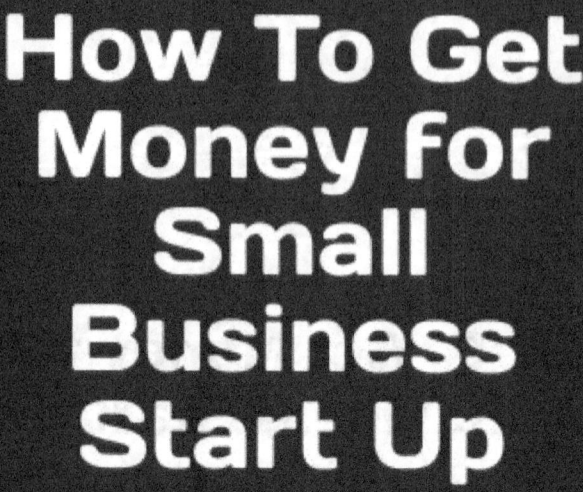

How To Get Money for Small Business Start Up

How to Get Massive Money from Crowdfunding, Government Grants and Government Loans

Ramsey Colwell

By Ramsey Colwell

www.ingramcontent.com/pod-product-compliance
Lightning Source LLC
Chambersburg PA
CBHW052123070526
44586CB00016B/2058